Good Things TO KNOW

MICHAEL PHILLIPS

444 Common Sense Maxims for a Happy Life

Published by Bethany House Publishers
A Ministry of Bethany Fellowship, Inc.
6820 Auto Club Road, Minneapolis, Minnesota 55438

Printed in the United States of America

ISBN 1-55661-319-9

*T*O MY GOOD FRIEND ....

*P*RESENTED BY ....

*D*ATE ....

Introduction

I have three sons. For years I have been trying to convey to them, in a multitude of ways, the priorities and spiritual perspectives by which I attempt to order my life. My prayer has been that I would somehow be able to transmit my whole value system and outlook—my insights on what things are most valuable, how I view my surroundings and people and relationships, what things matter to me, the way I try to walk with God. If you have sons and daughters, I'm sure you share these goals.

Several years ago I began giving my boys some instruction in view of their approaching adulthood. We called these our "Fatherhood Lessons." This desire to prepare them for life shifted and took on added features when my wife and I expanded our home school to include a few other students in addition to our own three sons. I found myself thinking like a parent *and* a teacher, and thinking of my responsibilities toward young people who hadn't grown up with me, who did not know me deeply and personally, and who were from a different background than my sons.

I began writing some things down. When we traveled together as a school, we compiled a list of rules. They were not just *do's and don'ts* of conduct and behavior, but a whole outlook on life, relationships, dealing with conflict, attitudes toward learning, how to encounter new people and situations, etc. As we rode along in our van, we discussed all kinds of things, including our written "maxims," always with the end in mind of preparing these young people for their future lives and marriages and friendships and jobs.

What eventually emerged was an accumulation of brief statements and nuggets of advice to equip these teens to be men and women of integrity, character and solid relational fiber. It turned out, however, to be more than just a list of suggestions for young people, but rather a book—this book you are holding in your hand.

In the end I pray it will be valuable to you too, whatever your age and wherever you find yourself along life's journey. These are not just pieces of advice I have passed along to others, but daily reminders to myself about how I want to live.

You will probably not find yourself in agreement with everything I have to say, and your own life's experience will bring hundreds of your own maxims to mind. I encourage you to personalize this little book by jotting down your own favorite "good things" on the pages provided at the end.

I hope you find it interesting and beneficial, and perhaps something you will want to pass along to others.

—Michael Phillips

To the students of Sunrise Academy

I have always tried to teach you to think and to delve deeply into things. Now it's your turn to uncover the layers of meaning in these growth-producing proverbs. I think I can guarantee that they are indeed good things to know, and that following them will fill your days with purpose and accomplishment...and happiness!

Alaina, Jeriah, Gregory, Robin, Patrick...I love you all. I pray for God's best and fullest and richest for you. You are nearly men and women, nearly ready to extend your roots deep and stretch your wings and embark on your own life's adventures. I pray that what I have been able to give you, including the principles in these pages, will guide you toward godliness as you mature, and that you will find them valuable enough that someday you will want to pass them on to your own sons and daughters.

Blessings to you...from your dad and teacher.

1. Communicate with gracious words and phrases.

2. Say "I'm sorry" at least once a day.

3. Every person you meet knows something you don't. Discover what it is.

4. Do not exalt yourself.

5. Remain on the lookout for opportunities to praise someone for a job well done.

6. Smile a lot.

7. Be the first to extend your hand.

8. Eat fruit for breakfast. You'll have more energy running on a quarter tank than a full one.

9. Do your best. Not *the* best... *your* best.

10. Think in fours—the number of completion. To give the earth fullness and totality and breadth, God gave it four corners, four seasons, and divided the day into four phases. Make what you do full and complete.

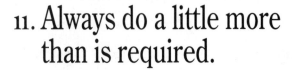

11. Always do a little more
than is required.

12. Know the book of Proverbs inside out.
    Read it often. Underline your favorites.

13. Look people in the eye.

14. Dream.

15. Get up and watch an occasional sunrise.

16. Wear slippers in the evening.

17. Get enough sleep, but not more than you need.

18. Whatever kind of exercise you choose, sweat a lot at least three times a week.

19. Take personal responsibility.

20. Watch Mr. Rogers, even after you're grown. Role models are becoming more and more difficult to find.

21. Remember people's birthdays.

22. Buy quality, but don't pay full price.

23. Don't chase fantasies.

24. If you put your foot in your mouth, humble yourself and take it out. Don't try to defend yourself and stick it in farther!

25. Keep a journal.

26. Take a walk in a warm rain.

27. Let integrity guide your steps and wisdom your decisions, not trying to figure every angle for your own gain.

28. Make truth your highest life priority. Not just knowing it, *living* it.

29. Look forward to being corrected. Handling such times graciously is the mark of a mature man or woman.

30. Know your favorite two roses by name. Cultivate them, and give away the flowers.

31. Say "Thank you" at least twice daily.

32. Fill your time purposefully, don't let it just sweep by you.

33. Pray for people you pass, even if you don't know them.

34. Get dirt on your hands as often as you have the chance.

35. Don't gossip. Never talk about others merely to give expression to your curiosity or someone else's.

36. Be scrupulously honest. Go out of your way to be truthful.

37. *Efficiency* is the key to getting things done, not having more time.

38. Watch movies and TV shows made before 1965.

39. Take an occasional cold shower just for the invigoration of it.

40. Clean out your gutters every fall.

41. Recognize body language in others that makes you feel small. Then get rid of all hints of such in yourself.

42. Don't be anxious to tell all you know.

43. If praise comes to you, let it be from a mouth other than your own.

44. Make your own bread.

45. Show appreciation chiefly for who people *are* rather than for what they have *done.* The latter, however, may be the doorway into the former.

46. Remind yourself of God's presence with you throughout all your activities.

47. Take time out during the evening to watch the sun set.

48. Set goals.

49. Carry them out.

50. Delight in wisdom.

51. Don't watch award shows, contemporary sit-coms, soaps, or quiz programs.

52. Buy what you need when it's on sale. Never buy what you *don't* need just because it's on sale.

53. Keep your workspace (desk, room, garage, kitchen, office, workbench) tidy.

54. Don't travel without jumper cables.

55. Make plans by seeking advice.

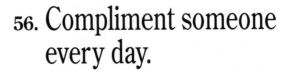

56. Compliment someone every day.

57. Dedicate yourself to quality.

58. Find five things every day to thank God for.

59. Read history.

60. Whatever your living-space limitations, grow something you can eat.

61. Go to a chiropractor.

62. Two secrets to financial success and independence: *Give* ten percent away (in service to the Lord and others); *Put* ten percent away (save for the future).

63. Have at least three favorite classical composers. Invest in their music and listen to it regularly.

64. Don't eat after 8:00 p.m.

65. Don't jump on bandwagons. Let things prove themselves, *then* get involved.

66. Take pictures.

67. Find an herb tea you like and drink it occasionally instead of coffee.

68. Don't compare your best with someone else's.

69. In making important decisions, don't worry about going slow. Remember: God is never in a hurry.

70. Keep your pencils sharpened.

71. Avoid strife. Walk
away from quarrels.

72. Walk in the sand barefoot every summer.

73. Take delight in doing things with your hands.

74. Wash your children's feet when they are growing up. They will remember it.

75. Avoid people who talk too much.

76. Put the most favorable construction on other people's words and deeds.

77. Have at least five favorite authors, representing fiction *and* non-fiction, past *and* contemporary.

78. When you start something, finish it. A trail of half-finished projects and ideas gives way to random purposelessness.

79. Don't embark on something that's not worth doing.

80. Share your feelings with your family.

81. Take vitamins.

82. Everyone possesses the same twenty-four hours. Use them well.

83. Be slow to speak of what you are "going to do." Let results tell the tale.

84. Convey enthusiasm whether you feel it or not.

85. Keep reading two books at the same time.

86. Never defend yourself immediately. Begin by taking the blame upon yourself. Be extremely reluctant to conclude that a defense is needed. If it is, respond graciously and appropriately at a later time.

87. Don't take yourself too seriously.

88. Learn to juggle.

89. Read a novel by the light of a fire and the crackling of its logs.

90. Do your taxes in February.

91. Fill your car's gas tank when the gauge is at one-quarter.

92. Establish a yearly tradition that you do individually with each of your children.

93. Separate Spring and Easter. Celebrate new growth, flowers, bunnies, and chocolate on the first day of Spring. Celebrate Jesus' resurrection on Easter.

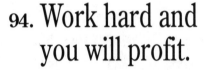

94. Work hard and you will profit.

95. When the sun is not out, let your face act as sunshine to those around you.

96. Laugh at your own foibles.

97. Smile at others in a traffic jam. It will be a balm in the midst of an impersonal and hectic world.

98. Look for nature's personality. Everything bears the fingerprint of God.

99. Say what you mean and mean what you say. Let your *yes* be yes, and your *no* be no. Shoot your arrows straight.

100. Limit your intake of red meat and milk. You'll live longer and the years will contain more energy.

101. Have a firm yet sensitive and sincere handshake.

102. Blessed is the man or woman who knows how to listen.

103. Go walking in a storm with someone you love.

104. Whenever you encounter a grumpy or sour person, determine immediately to draw a smile out of them before the interaction is over.

105. Read to your children.

106. Take a few two-lane roads instead of the interstate.

107. About procrastination...what you have to do, do it *now*.

108. Notice little things. Sometimes they really do speak the loudest.

109. Find ways to deny your *self* what it wants. The key to maturity is found in Mark 8:34.

110. Remember George MacDonald's words: "Men would understand; they do not care to obey. They try to understand where it is impossible they should understand except by obeying."

111. Don't complain.

112. Control what comes into your mind.

113. Save for what you want, then buy it. Don't buy first and try to pay later.

114. Walk tall.

115. Watch reruns of "Little House on the Prairie" and discuss its values as a family.

116. Approach most encounters assuming the other person is smarter than you.

117. Celebrate May Day. Nobody else does, but good traditions are hard to find and shouldn't be let go of easily. Make May baskets. Give flowers.

118. Stand up when greeting or being introduced to someone.

119. Remain open and eager for new ideas.

120. Read Oswald Chambers' classic, *My Utmost for His Highest.*

121. Make people feel important, but don't flatter.

122. Invest in music lessons. Drive an old car and buy fewer clothes, if necessary, to pay for them.

123. When you go to Disneyland, ride the Storybook Canal Boat instead of Space Mountain.

124. Never squelch an idea someone is excited about.

125. Spread jelly on Waverly Wafers.

126. When you see something your husband or wife would like, buy it. Keep a private stash of potential gifts hidden away for special occasions, or to give for no occasion. Don't let birthdays and anniversaries wait till the last minute.

127. Always roll up your own sleeping bag. Roll it tight.

128. Don't be afraid to say, "I don't know." People can smell a bluff a mile away.

129. Pray for wisdom daily.

130. Don't assume people remember you. Say your name as you shake hands, even if you've met the person before.

131. When you answer the phone, make sure the other person feels the smile in your voice.

132. When evaluating new involvements, ask how you will view its importance when lying on your deathbed.

133. Develop inner eyesight. Everything has multiple layers of meaning and purpose.

134. Remain vigilantly on the lookout for potential accident situations.

135. When walking, biking, driving, or running, don't trust the other guy.

136. Drive defensively. Assume other drivers will *not* do as they should.

137. Make sure everyone in the car is wearing seat belts—always.

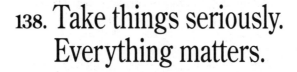

138. Take things seriously.
Everything matters.

139. Go out of your way to expose your children to wise men and women whose values will rub off on them (Proverbs 13:20).

140. Lose no opportunity to develop relationships with wise men and women whose outlook will rub off on *you*.

141. If you watch TV, keep a mute switch in your hand. Don't watch ads. Screen out anything you don't think Jesus would watch.

142. Make family birthdays count. Build memories.

143. Set about your work vigorously and with a cheerful spirit.

144. Don't offer counsel to someone who doesn't want it.

145. Take your family to the nursery and let everyone buy a new plant.

146. Walk in the woods.

147. When you're on a trip, stop and take time to climb someplace high.

148. Be willing to admit, "I need some help."

149. Don't let advertisers have their way with you.

150. Know your neighbors.

151. Have a will. Keep it current.

152. When in doubt, hold your tongue. Don't forget what Solomon said: When words are many, sin is not absent.

153. Draw out those who are less talkative.

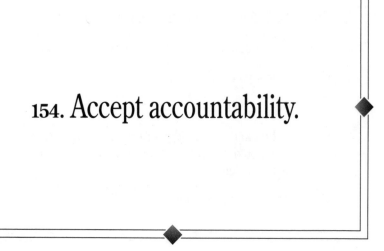

154. Accept accountability.

155. Pay attention to details. They are the mortar that holds together life's bricks.

156. Take a class in music appreciation.

157. Lavishly display pictures of those you love.

158. When someone new moves into your block, take them a fresh loaf of homemade bread and welcome them to the neighborhood.

159. Don't talk about the family things you want to do "someday." Do them.

160. In *everything*—do as
you would have done
to you.

161. Invest in lives first, God's work second, and assets last. Always keep in mind those things that will endure for eternity.

162. Save the cards from your children and spouse. Give them a place of honor.

163. Seek no recognition by men.

164. Leave the care of your life in the hands of the Father.

165. Whether you camp or not, consider yourself an outdoor person. The outdoors, after all, is God's house. Be at home in it.

166. Pray for your children every night after they're asleep.

167. Prioritize activities with this test: Will it matter five years from now?

168. Write letters of appreciation when you have been treated well.

169. Don't paint over natural wood grain.

170. Appreciate old things—barns, books, houses, clothes, furniture, movies...even ideas.

171. If you find yourself saying, "That's good enough," it probably isn't.

172. Arrive two to five minutes ahead of time.

173. Empty the garbage before it overflows.

174. Don't put bumper stickers on your car.

175. Put on Christlikeness,
whether you are worthy
of the garment or not.

176. On the job, whatever your position, make yourself indispensable.

177. Remember that it's possible to say "I'm sorry" no matter who's wrong. They are powerful words for the reconciliation and healing of differences.

178. Help clean up.

179. All other things being equal, go for the natural, the organic, the earthy, the old, the agrarian, the rural, the wholesome.

180. Never make excuses.

181. Put the toilet lid down.

182. Learn to identify and use soft phrases such as "Would you like...?" instead of "Do you want...?"

183. Be curious.

184. The secret of happiness lies not in doing what you like but in liking what you have to do.

185. Be decisive. You'll goof sometimes, but being capable of making decisions will strengthen your fiber.

186. Make MacDonald's quest, *Discovering the Character of God,* the quest of your life.

187. Read good books again. Reread a favorite from childhood.

188. View problems as opportunities. Trials are the norm and the raw material of growth.

189. Go to the grocery store when you're *not* hungry.

190. Always shake hands with the winner after you've lost a game, giving them a bright smile and genuine compliment.

191. Approach most encounters assuming the other person is smarter than you.

192. If you aspire to being an employer someday, be a faithful employee.

193. Keep your projections modest. Always deliver more than you promise.

194. Don't let the world squeeze you into its mold.

195. Don't let the Christian world squeeze you into its mold.

196. Don't let peers squeeze you into their mold. Be true to your own values.

197. Be a door-opener in other people's lives.

198. Go to small-town fairs and celebrations.

199. Pay bills early in the month.

200. Maintain order in all aspects of your life.

201. Make your word, even on the smallest matter, solid as a million-dollar collateral.

202. When you're angry, slow down and do nothing.

203. Be the one to install a fresh roll of toilet paper.

204. Make sure your children know which are your favorite books.

205. Find originality within yourself and cultivate it.

206. Wherever you go and however high you climb, never forget your roots.

207. Remember your manners. Wherever you are, behave as if you're at the White House.

208. Sing the *old* songs.

209. Don't win games more than a third of the time.

210. Lend your books liberally, but keep track of them ruthlessly.

211. Give gifts you have made with your own hands.

212. Make some *thing* that becomes a regular part of your household furniture, even if it's a crude bench or a barrel cut in half and filled with a plant. Your family should grow up using something you made.

213. Take a family picture every year.

214. Make sure other people don't have to pick up after you.

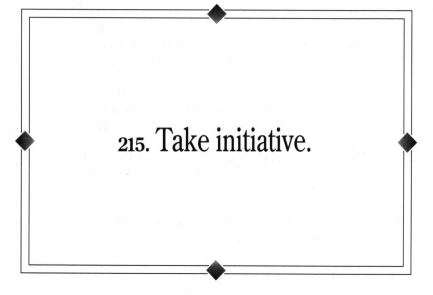

215. Take initiative.

216. Get inside other people's skin. See things through their eyes, seek to understand their point of view.

217. Fix leaky faucets after two weeks, not six months.

218. Never talk about people critically unless you're a direct part of the problem or the potential solution.

219. Read the small print. Be slow to commit yourself financially.

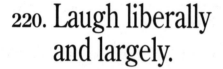

220. Laugh liberally
and largely.

221. Browse used bookstores. A used book has more experience than a new one.

222. Leave things in better condition than you found them.

223. Don't let the antifreeze in your car get rusty.

224. Plan ahead. (Not very original, but as important as ever.)

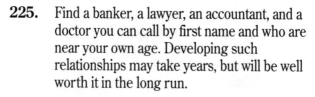

225. Find a banker, a lawyer, an accountant, and a doctor you can call by first name and who are near your own age. Developing such relationships may take years, but will be well worth it in the long run.

226. Always look at both sides.

227. Watch "The Great Race" with your family. Laugh hard.

228. If you trust someone enough to ask for their advice, take it. It's insulting to ask for a recommendation you don't intend to take.

229. Don't talk about yourself.

230. Always make a clear distinction between opinions and truth. Don't assume *your* opinions are automatically the latter.

231. Go Christmas caroling together. Invite another family.

232. Make Micah 6:8 your life's goal: To do justice, to love kindness, and to walk humbly with your God.

233. Celebrate the lives of elderly loved ones. Give them a birthday party with testimonials. They won't be with you forever. It's too late if approbations aren't given until the funeral.

234. If someone confides in you, keep a secret.

235. If you're on a diet, don't tell anyone. Let them see the results.

236. Don't let the phone rule your life.

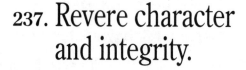

237. Revere character and integrity.

238. Know how to change tires and fix leaky radiator hoses.

239. Visit elderly people, especially in your neighborhood.

240. Don't top someone else's story.

241. Keep tabs on what you borrow. Return the item the minute you're done with it and in as good or better condition.

242. Read C. S. Lewis's *Mere Christianity* once every three years.

243. Every day look for some little thing you can improve about how you do your job.

244. Express contrary views without being contrary or divisive. Leave people thinking, "Wow, that was a pleasant conversation," even though different perspectives may have been aired.

245. Be prepared for Jesus to come back tomorrow. Go about your work as if it will be two hundred years.

246. Try to outdo others only in this: humility and service to others.

247. Find good men and women to emulate.

248. Have coffee tables you can put your feet on.

249. Carry no grudges. They'll weigh you down more than a fifty-pound pack.

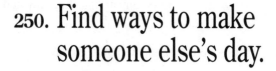

250. Find ways to make someone else's day.

251. Squander no opportunities to express gratefulness, esteem or love.

252. Keep your problems to yourself, draw other people's problems out. Be sympathetic with theirs, don't bore them with yours.

253. Whatever happens, give thanks.

254. Be an example.

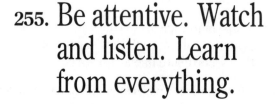

255. Be attentive. Watch and listen. Learn from everything.

256. Keep the flow going. Find hundreds of ways to give. The flow *into* your life is through the same pipe as the *outflow* into the lives of others. The volume of blessings *in* equals the volume *out*.

257. Find ways to refresh others.

258. Life is full of molehills that look like mountains to many. Walk right on past them, even though others have stopped to put on their mountain-climbing equipment.

259. Keep your sights fixed in the distance, and your hands busy up close.

260. Read Henry Drummond's *The Greatest Thing in the World* often.

261. Never let yourself spiritualize not doing something you just plain ought to do.

262. Take responsibility for every area of your life.

263. Look at the past, learn from it, then move on.

264. Every several years, pretend you're dirt poor and do Christmas the old-fashioned-way—one present each, no money spent, everything handmade. They will probably be your most memorable Christmases.

265. Send cards of encouragement and friendship. Everyone needs doses of love.

266. Never invoke God's leading to mask personal ambition or recklessness.

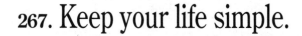

267. Keep your life simple.

268. Treat your family to Chinese food at home in little white cartons.

269. Bigger is not necessarily better. Look for the "better" in the small, the quiet, the still, the obscure.

270. Put your favorite quotes up on the wall.

271. Be a peacemaker.

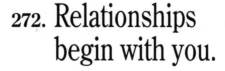

272. Relationships
begin with you.

273. Have a few collections, whether it be seashells or cow mugs, old books or stamps. As your children grow older, give them your special things as little pieces of yourself.

274. Never make light of another's good intentions.

275. Don't enter into a business deal with someone who has nothing to lose.

276. Surprise your family by taking them out to breakfast.

277. Minimize the importance of personal viewpoint. Stress *what's* right rather than *who's* right.

278. Be positive! See the glass as half full—even when it looks half empty.

279. Keep your own counsel until it is time to speak. Loose tongues have perpetrated more mischief among Christians than many of the Devil's schemes.

280. Never presume on another's kindness. Don't mooch or take advantage.

281. Stop grumpiness in its tracks with your own cheerfulness.

282. Find ways to do good to your adversaries.

283. Put travel posters and maps on the wall. Keep your worldview expansive.

284. On the job, think like an owner.

285. Do good deeds that will never be seen by anyone.

286. Don't let your hands become soft. Keep some calluses around.

287. Let no sharp, confrontive, or ungracious words pass your lips.

288. Don't take eight minutes to do every five-minute job. It could result in ten or fifteen wasted years of your life.

289. Make your *no's* so gracious they feel like *yes's*.

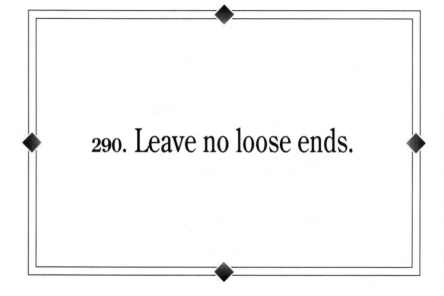

290. Leave no loose ends.

291. Don't walk by things that need to be done. Take care of them.

292. Never force people to wait for you.

293. Make people feel better at the end of an interaction with you than they did at its beginning.

294. Build on your strengths. Use them to serve others.

295. Build on your weaknesses. Work to overcome them. Turn them into strengths.

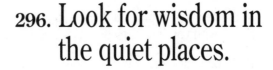

296. Look for wisdom in the quiet places.

297. Personalize your boss's priorities. If you can't make them your own, you will eventually become a liability.

298. Be cautious around people who are always "into" some great new thing every time you see them. Steadiness and consistency get the job done.

299. Call a friend and ask if there is any project around the house he or she hasn't been able to get to and would like some help with.

300. Go after excellence.

301. If you broke it, fix it. If you can't, get it fixed.

302. Make your mistakes. Learn from them. Cry your tears. Then get up and move on.

303. Give your best to others. Building visions and needs into people's lives is the best investment you'll make. This is especially true when it comes to employers and family members.

304. Store up the commands of Scripture within you.

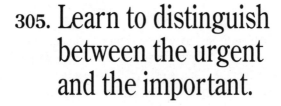

305. Learn to distinguish between the urgent and the important.

306. Don't get heavily involved in church leadership until your own family is grown.

307. Plant fruit trees when you move into a new house.

308. Tell your family you're taking them out to dinner. An hour ahead of time, pile everybody into the car and drive to the store. Let everyone pick out a TV dinner. Enjoy them along with a '50s movie.

309. Don't fill up conversational air space with mere chatter. Quiet between friends is sometimes a good and rich thing.

310. Be lenient and forgiving, but prudent. Give people a second chance. Not a fourth.

311. Learn to love hardship and personal discipline. They are ingredients of maturity and inner strength.

312. Let knowledge come *into* you in greater measure than you speak it *out*. This is one case where the inflow should be greater than the outflow.

313. There's one thing you can never get back—the words that just left your lips. Don't utter them carelessly.

314. Enjoy something sweet. Keep a sense of humor about dieting.

315. Never invoke grace to cover irresponsibility.

316. Gather around you people you deeply trust. Lean on them for counsel. Many advisors make success all the more likely.

317. Make and save money a little at a time. Don't go after a "killing." Steady and slow wins the race.

318. Find the balance between openness and skepticism. Both are required in the search for truth.

319. Pray daily: "Lord, show me what you want me to do. Help me to do it."

320. Listen to advice, however it comes to you and even if wrongly motivated. There is food to be gleaned from the most unlikely sources.

321. Be a skilled listener.

322. When challenged, respond with soft-spoken gentleness. Harsh words only stir up more anger.

323. Do something crazy with your family. Your children will treasure the memories of you goofing off and acting like a kid with them.

324. Go overboard with kindness. The excess is never wasted.

325. Cultivate a few deep friendships rather than a hundred casual acquaintances.

326. Play Monopoly.

327. Do not pray for something unless you are willing to be part of the answer.

328. Don't gullibly believe everything you hear. At the same time, be willing to find truth from any source.

329. Seek truth.

330. Make this an automatic response: When given a gruff look, throw back a wide smile.

331. As soon as it starts to rain, go outside and smell the pavement.

332. Look for and dig out sources of pride within yourself.

333. Don't let any "thing" consume you—especially a computer.

334. Never make another person the butt of a joke.

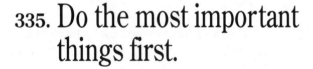

335. Do the most important things first.

336. Weigh your answers before speaking.

337. Surround yourself with persons of noble character.

338. Make the Scripture deeply personal: "Search me, O God, and know my heart." Keep your spiritual basements and gutters cleaned out, as well as those of your house.

339. Learn to identify those areas of coveting in your life. We all do it. It's just that most people haven't learned to identify it in themselves.

340. When things are the hardest, that's when they count the most.

341. Take family walks in the evening.

342. Eschew fashions. Dress without calling attention to yourself.

343. Don't monopolize conversations.

344. Settle disputes promptly.

345. Say nothing you wouldn't be willing for Jesus to hear. He's right beside you in all conversations.

346. Put the lids back on felt-tip pens.

347. Conquer drift and futility. Make your days count.

348. The externals of your life (yard, car, house, habits, desk, words, dress, mannerisms) reflect your inner self.

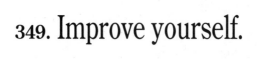

349. Improve yourself.

350. Encourage correspondence with lots of pen pals.

351. Get things down in writing.

352. Make sure the lasting legacy of your life is godliness, not a list of assets and accomplishments.

353. Never borrow life's necessities. If you must borrow, make sure it is an investment that has a solid return.

354. There's one thing you'll never have again—the present moment. Use it wisely.

355. Keep copies of the letters you write.

356. Don't go to the mall to hang around. Conduct your business and go home.

357. Don't rush. Most things will wait. Hastiness breeds inefficiency.

358. Pray for people in the news facing tragedy.

359. Avoid what's "in."

360. Don't be quick to assume the obvious. There's more to most things than meets the eye—people, roses, circumstances, and decisions. Everything has roots.

361. Summon the courage to take a stand.

362. Don't forget the mark of a Christian. The identifying badge we are to wear is love, not a lapel pin.

363. Stop at roadside produce stands. Buy things as close to the source as possible.

364. Be a learner. Add
to your learning.

365. Anticipate each day and the experiences it will bring like a classroom. Look forward to learning something new.

366. Turn your *thinks* into *things*—give spiritual faith practical teeth.

367. When you have decided on a major purchase, wait a week before you buy. Sometimes things aren't all they seem at first. A bit of reflection is always positive.

368. Remember the proverb:
Though it cost you all
you have, get wisdom.

369. Honor unknown heroes who display character and integrity instead of the world's celebrities.

370. Keep your awareness quotient at peak operational capacity.

371. Think of the things you'll look back on at 80 and wish you'd done more of. Do one of those things today.

372. When introduced to someone new, try to use his or her name immediately.

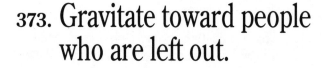

373. Gravitate toward people who are left out.

374. Drain the dishwater when it loses its suds, and run a new batch.

375. Plan to visit Europe. Maybe you will, maybe you won't, but the dream counts for more than you may realize.

376. Remain constantly on the lookout for ways to bring increased organization into your routine and habit patterns.

377. Don't look to others to cover for you. You are responsible.

378. Make your witness visual, not verbal.

379. Keep your car tuned and the oil fresh.

380. Keep your inner streams flowing. Allow no stagnant pools to develop.

381. Never let yourself drift into making spirituality abstract.

382. Have a reason for what you say. Don't just air opinions at random.

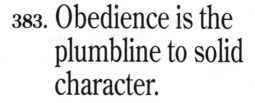

383. Obedience is the plumbline to solid character.

384. Follow through on commitments you make, no matter how small. Don't ever say you will do something and then not do it.

385. Give others the same grace you know you need.

386. Don't commit to something that will take time away from things of higher priority.

387. Practice the Proverbs.

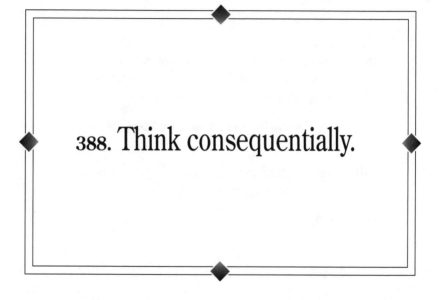

388. Think consequentially.

389. Consider the natural outgrowths of your actions: If I do this, what will be the repercussions—to myself and others—both immediately and in the long range?

390. On normal days, don't wear a tie or heels after 6:00 p.m.

391. Spend a little more to patronize the local family store instead of the big chain.

392. If you have a dog, carry a plastic bag and clean up its messes.

393. When making friends,
look for character.

394. Do the dishes more than just occasionally for your wife.

395. Occasionally get an annoying house repair taken care for your husband.

396. Keep focused.

397. Have the person whose birthday it is give the presents.

398. Resist the temptation to tell people about your favorite Gary Larson cartoon. Some things—Far Sides and spiritual truths—have to be experienced firsthand.

399. On evenings and Sunday afternoons, wear faded jeans and a sweat shirt.

400. Do only those things you would want Jesus to participate in with you.

401. It is impossible to be perfect, yet Jesus commanded us to be perfect. In the balance between these two facts lie huge but largely unseen secrets of the Christian life.

402. Respect other people's space.

403. Don't limit yourself to the stereotypes of your gender.

404. Take the low road. Don't grab the best seat.

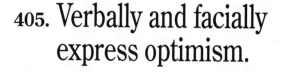

405. Verbally and facially express optimism.

406. Great insight into the be-perfect-in-the-midst-of-our-imperfection enigma can be found in MacDonald's statement: God is easy to please, and hard to satisfy.

407. Whatever the assignment, do it with gusto and diligence.

408. Never forget that spirituality is *DO,* not know...and especially not just *say.* Principles and truths have meaning only as they grow out of actions.

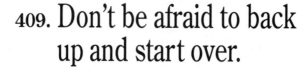

409. Don't be afraid to back up and start over.

410. Don't embark on something you haven't thought through.

411. Enjoy salads.

412. Have courage to take the narrow road.

413. Have your suitcases packed and be ready to walk out the door 24 hours before a trip. On ones of two weeks or more, make it 48 hours.

414. Smell roses in the summer, decaying leaves in the fall, approaching stormclouds in winter, and hyacinths every spring.

415. Make pizza together as a family activity. Get an old movie. Stuff yourselves.

416. Don't go to a movie without great caution. Be prepared to get up and leave at a second's notice if there are sexual innuendoes or undue profanity.

417. Walk to your own drumbeat.

418. Have a guest room. Cultivate the ministry of hospitality in your home.

419. In all situations, be polite.

420. Find opportunities to give gifts in secret.

421. In a mutual encounter, be the one to speak out with the first greeting.

422. Punch in *before* you are expected, and punch out *after* quitting time.

423. Watch old Roy Rogers westerns. Enjoy the music.

424. Know your own motives. Such requires honest introspection. Better to be too hard on yourself than to let yourself off the hook prematurely.

425. Don't give in to the cravings of your soul.

426. Leave the bathroom sink cleaner than you found it.

427. Engage in no doctrinal disputations.

428. Pray daily: "Lord, show me who you want me to be. Help me be it."

429. Invite a diverse group of people over on a Sunday afternoon and watch them interact with one another. Unity among God's people needs down-to-earth doing.

430. Do what is before you to do not for the recognition of others but for the sheer satisfaction and integrity of work well done.

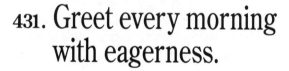

431. Greet every morning
with eagerness.

432. Praise people—especially your children—in front of others.

433. Speak words of honor about your husband or wife in front of others.

434. Go to Marie Callender's and enjoy a slice of peanut butter pie.

435. Seek no honor.

436. Think of yourself as creative. We all are. That's how God made us—in His image. But that creativity takes a million different forms, and we each have to discover our own.

437. Make the bed and put away your clothes.

438. Invest in a modest whole-life insurance policy when you're young. If you're not young, put it off no longer.

439. Familiarize yourself with tools. Get your own set. Know how to use them.

440. Keep your yard trim and its plants groomed.

441. Hide a key somewhere on your car.

442. Be your husband or wife's best friend.

443. Don't set a goal unless
you plan to reach it.

444. Bring the thoughts of your mind, the tasks of your hands, and the expression of your personhood to fulfillment. Two hands plus two feet equals four. Mind, soul, body, spirit equals four. The Father, the Son, the Holy Spirit and I equals four. Make these three groupings of completion—444—representative of a life well lived in the principles of the Kingdom.

GOOD THINGS TO KNOW

GOOD THINGS TO KNOW

GOOD THINGS TO KNOW

Good Things To Know

Good Things To Know

GOOD THINGS TO KNOW